This Book Belongs To

____

____

____

COPYRIGHT 2020

A NOTE FROM THE PUBLISHER

Hi. I am the owner at the Color publishing house that brought you this book. I hope, more than anything, that your child enjoyed this book. If they did, please consider leaving a review It takes a few minutes, but it would be so much appreciated. Reviews are a brilliant thing for small businesses like mine - they are the best way to let other potential
customers know about the book. I also want to create content for kids to enjoy it will always be incredibly helpful to hear what other parents are looking for. Other people's books have always inspired and entertained me and I hope that my kids' books can do the same.

a a a a a a a

a a a a a a a

A B C D E F G H I J K L M N O P Q R S T U V W X Y Z

𝓑 𝓑 𝓑 𝓑 𝓑 𝓑

𝒷 𝒷 𝒷 𝒷 𝒷 𝒷

C C C C C C

c c c c c c c

$\mathcal{D}$ $\mathcal{D}$ $\mathcal{D}$ $\mathcal{D}$ $\mathcal{D}$ $\mathcal{D}$

d d d d d d

$\mathcal{E}$ $\mathcal{E}$ $\mathcal{E}$ $\mathcal{E}$ $\mathcal{E}$ $\mathcal{E}$

e e e e e e

A B C D E F G H I J K L M N O P Q R S T U V W X Y Z

H H H H H H H H H H H

h h h h h h h h h h h

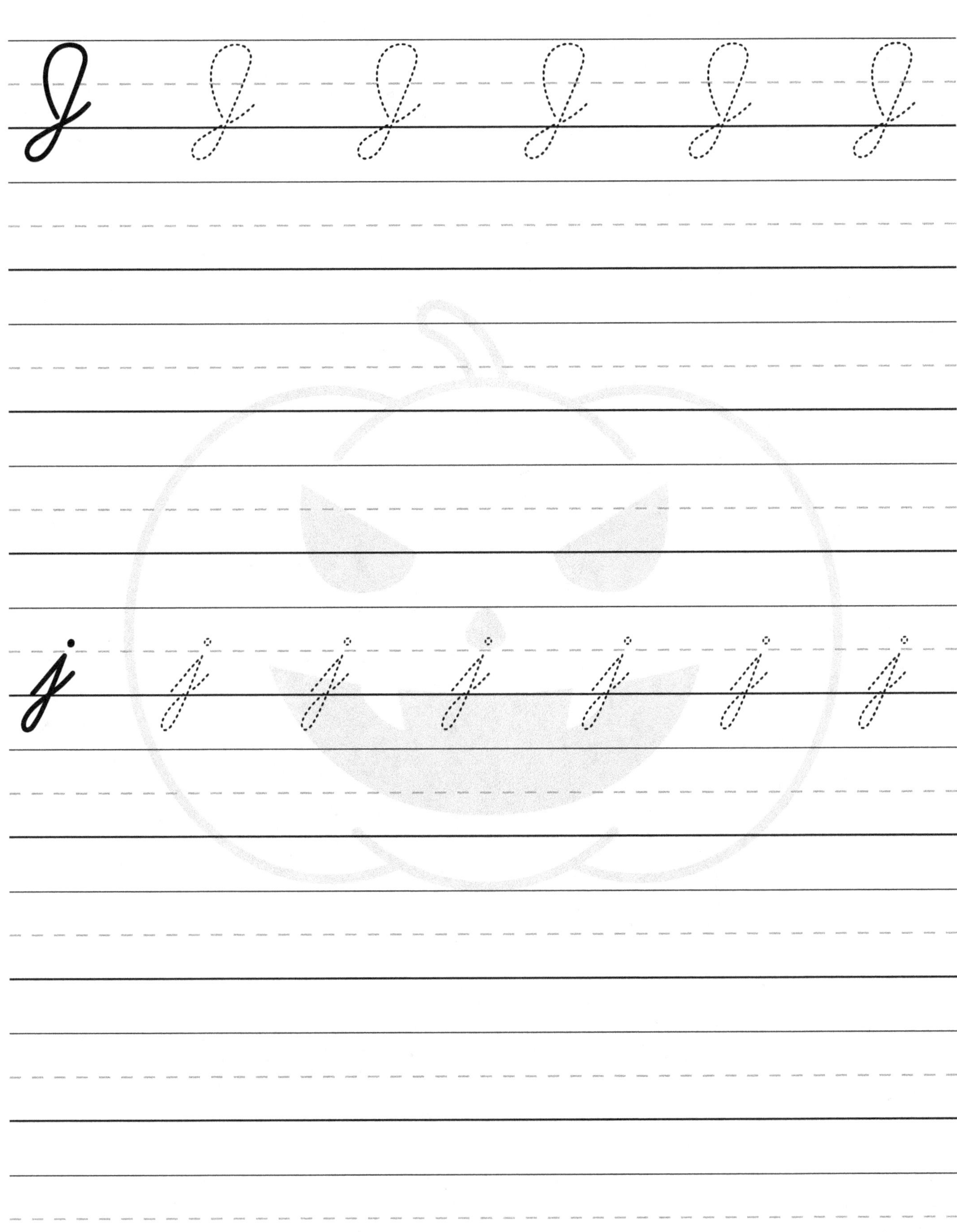

O O O O O O

o o o o o o

Q Q Q Q Q

q q q q q q

A B C D E F G H I J K L M N O P Q R **S** T U V W X Y Z

T T T T T T

t t t t t t

$\mathcal{V}$ $\mathcal{v}$ $\mathcal{v}$ $\mathcal{v}$ $\mathcal{v}$ $\mathcal{v}$ $\mathcal{v}$

$\mathcal{v}$ $\mathcal{v}$ $\mathcal{v}$ $\mathcal{v}$ $\mathcal{v}$ $\mathcal{v}$ $\mathcal{v}$

A B C D E F G H I J K L M N O P Q R S T U V W X Y Z

Y Y Y Y Y Y

y y y y y y

Ghost

Ghost   *Ghost*   *Ghost*

Spider

Spider *Spider* *Spider*

Witch

Pumpkin *Pumpkin*

Happy Halloween

Happy Halloween

Treat Or Trick

Treat Or Trick

Be afraid Be very afraid

Be afraid Be very

afraid

Space to write and draw yours own spooky words and sentences

Space to write and draw yours own spooky words and sentences

Space to write and draw yours own spooky words and sentences

Space to write and draw yours own spooky words and sentences

Space to write and draw yours own spooky words and sentences

Space to write and draw yours own spooky words and sentences

Space to write and draw yours own spooky words and sentences

Space to write and draw yours own spooky words and sentences

Space to write and draw yours own spooky words and sentences

Space to write and draw yours own spooky words and sentences

Space to write and draw yours own spooky words and sentences

Space to write and draw yours own spooky words and sentences

Space to write and draw yours own spooky words and sentences

Space to write and draw yours own spooky words and sentences

Space to write and draw yours own spooky words and sentences

Space to write and draw yours own spooky words and sentences

Space to write and draw yours own spooky words and sentences

Space to write and draw yours own spooky words and sentences

Space to write and draw yours own spooky words and sentences